The Penitential Psalms Today

A Journey with Psalms 6, 32, 38, 51, 102, 130 and 143

Mark J Whiting
Elder of QE Park Baptist Church, Guildford
and Reader at the University of Surrey

GROVE BOOKS LIMITED
RIDLEY HALL RD CAMBRIDGE CB3 9HU

Contents

Dedication
To my parents, Anne and Richard, for ceaseless encouragement.

Acknowledgments
I am very grateful for the immense patience and constructive criticism of the Grove Biblical Studies team.

First Impression March 2022
ISSN 1365-490X
ISBN 978 1 78827 223 0

1 Introducing the Penitential Psalms

The penitential psalms are an ancient group of seven psalms, numbered 6, 32, 38, 51, 102, 130 and 143 in most modern English Bibles.[1] This booklet is written with the conviction that these seven psalms are an undervalued resource in today's church. This chapter examines the prominent role of these psalms in personal devotion, doctrine, liturgy, preaching and poetry over the centuries.

Chapters two, three and four examine the penitential psalms in canonical order. These three chapters are structured so as to draw attention to Psalm 51 which we shall see can be understood as the penitential psalm *par excellence*. The concluding fifth chapter examines various ways in which these seven psalms can be used today. Whilst this book can be used at any time of year it will become apparent that a personal focus, or series of group studies, on these psalms is especially appropriate during the season of Lent.

Their Origin: Augustine and Cassiodorus

Prior to modern critical efforts to classify the psalms, two groups of psalms emerged many centuries ago. One group are the gradual psalms or psalms of ascents. These are the fifteen consecutive psalms—Psalm 120 to Psalm 134—each headed 'a song of ascents.' The second ancient group are the penitential psalms, with which this booklet is concerned. Their collective label within the Western Christian tradition dates to around the time of Saint Augustine (354–430 CE). He is often said to have been the first to group these seven psalms together. This is because of the centrality of penitence—showing sorrow for sin—found in his interpretation of these psalms. Whether they were understood as a group by Augustine is unclear, however, although his interpretation of these psalms certainly informed subsequent penitential interpretation. The first extant reference to them as a coherent group is in the work of Cassiodorus (c 485–c 585 CE).[2] In his large exegetical work, *The Expositions of the Psalms*, he examines all 150 psalms.[3] Each time he covers one of the penitential psalms he makes this designation clear and argues that there is a logical progression through the seven, from Psalm 6 to Psalm 143.

Their Use in the Medieval Period: Penance and Purgatory

The works of Augustine and Cassiodorus continued to inform psalm commentaries in the early Middle Ages.[4] By the eleventh century, lay commentaries on the seven penitential psalms were being made available across Europe. The most famous English example is Dame Eleanor Hull's (c 1390–1460) translation of a now lost twelfth-century French work.[5] This work was part of a wider movement, from the mid-thirteenth to the mid-sixteenth century, that saw the penitential psalms popularized in works known as Books of Hours.[6] These books were designed to be a primer for the personal faith development of lay people. They became the bestsellers of their day when books become readily available, initially printed and illustrated using woodcuts and, a little later, made by printing presses.[7] The accompanying images often featured episodes from the life of King David. A scene of him spying on the bathing Bathsheba featured especially prominently. Given the act of adultery and murder that followed, it might seem odd that David was understood as a moral exemplar in the Middle Ages. This was because of the contrition—the state of heartfelt penitence—that was understood to have followed his misdemeanours. The penitential psalms, and most famously Psalm 51, were understood as David's prayerful response to his sin.

Over time, each of the seven psalms was associated with one of the seven deadly sins.[8] This was complemented by doctrinal development that saw the origin and evolution of the sacrament of penance. This approach to addressing sin developed from the perceived need to formalize the process of forgiveness for post-baptismal sins. Praying the penitential psalms was one of several prescribed acts of penance assigned by a priest following absolution. The formalization of penance and the doctrine of purgatory led to the centrality of the penitential psalms in religious practice—reciting the penitential psalms was said to reduce the soul's time in purgatory.

During the Middle Ages, Lent took on greater prominence in the Christian liturgical year. It was a time for fasting and abstinence, as well as a season of focus on prayer and penitence. The penitential psalms featured prominently in many of the practices of Lent. Most famously of all, Pope Innocent III (c 1160–1216) proclaimed that all seven penitential psalms were to be prayed, whilst kneeling, throughout Lent, or at the very least on Lenten Fridays.[9]

Their Use at the Time of the Reformation: Luther and Fisher

The emergence of Protestantism and changes in Catholic theology during the Reformation, and in its immediate aftermath, saw a shift in the understanding and use of the penitential psalms. Luther found in the penitential psalms a piety that resonated strongly with his theology. The seven were so important to him that they were the subject, in 1517, of the first book that he personally saw through the printing press. This was a full six months before his more famous 'Ninety-five Theses.' Luther's *Die Sieben Bußpsalmen*, or *The Seven Penitential Psalms*, was reprinted several times and revised by him in 1525.

Luther's attraction to the penitential psalms probably lay with his sympathy to some of the concerns which motivated their grouping together. It has been suggested that there is (i) a connection between them and the theme of divine wrath, and (ii) a canonical connection with Paul's Letter to the Romans. Of the seven penitential psalms, three of them refer directly to divine anger or wrath (Pss 6.1, 38.1 and 102.10). The other four penitential psalms make no explicit comment about divine anger, although Ps 32.4 speaks of the experience of God's 'heavy hand.' Nevertheless, Paul's Letter to the Romans is recognized as the key place in the New Testament where God's wrath is a central concern. The early chapters of Romans make reference to the other four penitential psalms: Rom 3.4 quotes Ps 51.4; Rom 3.20 alludes to Ps 143.2; Rom 3.24 alludes to Ps 130.7 and Rom 4.7–8 quotes Ps 32.1–2.[10]

This relationship between these seven otherwise scattered psalms, and both Paul's Letter to the Romans and the theme of God's wrath is a complex theological one that unites the seven.[11] This is possibly why Martin Luther referred to four of the penitential psalms (32, 51, 130 and 143) as the 'Pauline Psalms.'[12]

For Luther much of the appeal of the penitential psalms was their use for personal devotion, and not just their synergy with his theology. He frequently interprets them with stark directness to his personal difficulties. In 1509 a contemporary of Luther's, the English bishop and cardinal, John Fisher (1469–1535), wrote a Catholic exposition of the penitential psalms. Fisher's concern, despite the large theological divide, also lay with these psalms as 'food for the soul.'[13]

The Seventeenth Century and Beyond: Preaching, Poetry and Music

After the Reformation these psalms found new roles in preaching, poetry and communal worship. The preacher, scholar and poet John Donne (1572–1631) had a love of the penitential psalms. His surviving corpus of sermons includes twenty-one on them—although all of his expositions are on the first four penitentials.[14] It would appear that this was an unfinished preaching project. Donne seems determined to find an alternative to the medieval use of these psalms—with the sermon affecting penitence rather than their recitation as penance.[15]

Donne's fellow Church of England priest and contemporary, George Herbert (1593–1633), was similarly influenced by the penitential psalms. These words from his poem *Home* exude the language of the penitentials as we will see in chapter two:

> Come Lord, my head doth burn, my heart is sick,
> While thou dost ever, ever stay:
> Thy long deferrings wound me to the quick,
> My spirit gaspeth night and day.
> O show thyself to me,
> Or take me up to thee![16]

The use of the penitential psalms in corporate worship differed among the diverse streams of Christianity that emerged from the religious turmoil of the sixteenth century. The reformed churches and non-conformist traditions tended to use them in metrical form as part of their commitment to singing all of the psalms. The Anglican church made specific use of the penitential psalms on Ash Wednesday, the start of Lent. For example, in the 1662 *Book of Common Prayer* Psalms 6, 32 and 38 are prescribed at matins. Psalm 51 is an office reading for the day, and then, at evensong Psalms 102, 130 and 143 are used.

In the Catholic church, in particular, more dramatic and innovative choral music evolved. One of the most famous and beautiful settings of a penitential psalm is Gregorio Allegri's (c 1582–1652) *Misere mei, Deus,* named after the Latin opening of Psalm 51. This work was written for use only in the Sistine Chapel during Holy Week. It has been said that the young Amadeus Mozart visited the chapel and was able to score the piece from memory, making its wider dissemination possible.[17] This work celebrates, through its ethereal beauty, the mercy shown to the penitent. A much more recent work, titled simply *Miserere,* by Arvo Pärt (1935–present) examines a different dynamic, that of fear when standing before a holy God at the last judgment. It begins with the Latin text of Psalm 51 sung one word at a time with a bassoon adding a solemn gap between each one. This ponderous frail cry is eventually met with a drum roll as the day of judgment arrives. These two works represent the immense spiritual and theological dynamic range of just one of the penitential psalms.

The penitential psalms continue to inspire musical works. For example, the contemporary English composer Howard Goodall produced an album of psalms with new musical settings in 2010 titled *Pelican in the Wilderness*. This includes three of the penitential psalms (Psalms 51, 102 and 130). Even in popular culture the reach of the penitentials is found in the form of Leonard Cohen's *Hallelujah*. This song can be understood as a riff on Psalm 51 given its reflection on David as the psalmist and the lyrical centrality of his fall on seeing Bathsheba bathing.

There is something of a gulf between the lengthy golden age in which these seven psalms eclipsed all others, and the present where they are more rarely celebrated as a group. As late as the mid-nineteenth century Neale and Littledale could meaningfully claim that the penitential psalms were:

> the seven weapons wherewith to oppose the seven deadly sins: the seven prayers inspired by the sevenfold Spirit to the repenting sinner: the seven guardians for the seven days of the week: the seven companions for the seven Canonical Hours of the day.[18]

There are many reasons why they were so central in the past and many more that might explain their wane. This booklet cannot hope to explore their complex history in depth. Our aim is rather more modest, to enable the reader to discover for themselves the role that these seven psalms might play in their personal devotion and community worship.

A Suggestion

This booklet refers to the NRSV and having this, or another modern translation to refer to is essential. In addition, I suggest that you also refer to another version of the Psalms as this can help make the poetic and metaphorical language of the psalms speak freshly. I personally have found that Robert Alter's translation works well in this regard.[19]

2

Psalms 6, 32 and 38: O Lord, Do Not Rebuke Me

This chapter examines the first three penitential psalms. Two of them, Psalms 6 and 38, open with the same words: 'O Lord, do not rebuke me.' In some liturgical contexts they are both known by their Latin opening words: *Domine, ne in furore*. These words provide a fitting subtitle for this chapter.

Psalm 6

At first sight this psalm seems to refer to the proverbial 'grave illness,' with its reference to shaking bones (Ps 6.2), wasting eyes (v 7), and a perceived nearness of death (v 5). The opening concern with a fear of God's anger (v 1) means the references to shaking bones and wasting eyes can be understood as physical illness, metaphorical allusions or psychosomatic symptoms. Luther (1483–1546) saw sin as the issue in this psalm and Calvin (1509–1564) took a similar line—understanding the physical ailments to be a consequence of anguish arising from fear of God.[20] Such a lens provides the traditional penitential stance for reading these seven psalms. In this way, the two Reformers essentially follow Augustine and Cassiodorus in connecting the psalmist's plight with sin. Such a reading is, of course, natural if the psalm has already been judged to be penitential. If the psalm is assessed on the basis of internal evidence only, and in its original context, then a different perspective is plausible. A case can be made that the psalmist's suffering, which includes acute illness (vv 6–7) and being taunted by enemies (vv 7–10), owes more to being a frail creature than an unrepentant sinner. Perhaps the psalmist is fearful of God's wrath in a manner more akin to Job? Perhaps they perceive God, in his anger, as inscrutable rather than as a purposeful judge of wrongdoing? A penitential interpretation is not the only one. We shall see, however, that the seven read together with such a lens have a compelling penitential synergy.

This psalm can be understood to comprise four short units or strophes: vv 1–3, vv 4–5, vv 6–7 and vv 8–10.[21] Verses 1–3 use parallelism—a rich poetic feature of Hebrew poetry which emphasizes key imagery—to draw attention to the psalmist's plight. The two lines of v 1 are twinned statements, with 1b articulating a fear of God's 'wrath' which builds on their concern of being rebuked in Yahweh's 'anger' in 1a. The beautifully balanced v 2 uses the divine name twice as the psalmist looks to Yahweh for grace and healing. Then v 3 jars with its concluding plaintive cry of, 'Yahweh—how long?' The second strophe, vv 4–5, intensifies the psalmist's plight. Death appears to be the likely outcome of their experience. The third strophe is a painful lament marked by hyperbole that capture the psalmist's tortured anguish. This desperate recollection of tears without end, and an accompanying loss of sight, is followed by resolution in the fourth strophe. As so often in the Psalms, there is a dramatic shift in mood. The psalmist's confidence that Yahweh has answered is a feature of the emphatic trust so prevalent in the psalter. This final section is addressed to the psalmist's enemies and functions as a testimony to God's faithfulness.

How does this psalm flow if we see it as a penitential psalm? In what might be termed a classical interpretation, the psalmist perceives God's anger as wrath that results from the antithesis between creaturely sinfulness and God's holiness. In understanding their sin and God's holy anger the poet is terrified. This is a depth of fear that is known deep inside one's bones (v 2), indeed in one's very soul (v 3), although Goldingay's alternative of 'whole being' is less anachronistic than 'soul' in its faithfulness to the Hebrew.[22] There is only one course of action. The psalmist has already turned from their sin, in coming before God, and now they ask God to turn towards them. They want deliverance from this terror and salvation from the grave. They spell out their plight to God with a sincerity that is evident in the copious tears that testify to an inner grief (vv 6–7). When their prayer is answered, the psalmist turns their attention to their enemies (v 9). Verse 10 is an expression of confident trust from the psalmist; a firm conviction that God will vindicate them. This anticipated outcome is twofold: the psalmist's enemies will know they were wrong and that they will experience a taste of the fear that the psalmist has been delivered from (vv 3, 10).

As our journey proceeds it will be apparent that some of the penitential psalms cohere with a penitential interpretation more readily than others. This is part of the larger issue of the profoundly open and generative richness of psalm imagery. The biblical psalms are open to multiple interpretations and this is an essential feature of their nature as poems and their veracity as prayers. Their penitential designation is the basis for one interpretive lens, and it is valuable in equipping us with rich prayer for the primary need of humanity: restoration and nurture of a living relationship with our creator.

Suggestions for Reflection and Discussion

- What angers God? In what sense, and to what extent, can God be understood to be angry with his people?
- To what extent can Luther's reading, of God disciplining or chastising the psalmist, be found here in Psalm 6?
- Having explored Psalm 6, what points of contact are there between it and the excerpt from George Herbert's poem quoted in section 1?

Psalm 32

This is the happiest of the seven psalms. It literally starts with the word 'happy' in some English translations (*eg* NRSV and GNT). In fact, both Ps 32.1 and v 2 start with this declaration. This happiness (Hebrew *'ašrê*) is richer than just conveying mood. It connotes a holistic and profound sense of well-being. This use of this word, as a 'beatitude,' echoes its use in the opening of the psalter (Ps 1.1). The lengthy Psalm 119 also starts with a paired use of this word. The happy tone of this psalm fits its modern label as an individual thanksgiving psalm. Its positive mood does not, however, make this a light psalm. The happiness has arisen only after sin and penitence, as is evident in Ps 32.5. Just as the opening is reminiscent of Psalms 1 and 119 so its conclusion echoes their concern with the fate of the wicked (Ps 32.10).

The large gap from Psalm 6 to Psalm 32 might appear to make a link between the first two penitential palms unlikely. Nevertheless, it will become apparent that Psalm 32's content makes sense as a step forward from Psalm 6. Psalm 32 also has several words, phrases and concerns linking it with Psalm 6. Note the wasting of bones and body in Ps 6.2, 6.7 and 32.3—this is typical language describing the plight of the suffering psalmist. We shall meet crushed and painful bones again in Pss 51.8 and 102.3.

Verse 3 explains that the issues the psalmist experienced arose from silence. To put this another way, the psalmist was suffering severe physical ailments because they were not listening to God's instruction nor were they confessing their sin to God. That unacknowledged sin is the issue is confirmed by Ps 32.5, on which this psalm turns. Here in a beautiful threefold parallelism of confessing sin, admitting iniquity and acknowledging transgression, the psalmist is forgiven. The progress from confession of sin to God's forgiveness happens without reference to the sacrificial system. This challenges the caricature of the lack of grace in the Old Testament. It is not surprising that the apostle Paul turns to this psalm in Rom 4.7–8 in his unpacking of the message of the gospel. Nor is it surprising that this psalm was so important for Augustine and Luther—Luther's doctrine of justification by faith fits coherently with the gracious forgiveness of God found here.

The penitential psalms are traditionally linked with the story of David, Bathsheba, and Uriah (2 Samuel 11–12) via the heading of the central psalm of the seven, Psalm 51, as we shall see in chapter three. The dramatic turn in Ps 32.5 from confession to forgiveness reflects the scene in 2 Sam 12.13:[23]

> David: 'I have sinned against the Lord.'
> Nathan: 'Now the Lord has put away your sin.'

Mercifully, God forgives our sin when we confess and ask forgiveness. Sadly, our sin can still have further consequences. This is apparent in the subsequent story in 2 Samuel and in our next psalm.

Ps 32.6 is an exhortation for others to follow the psalmist's example. A penitential reading is that confessed sin enables reconciliation of the penitent with God, and the result is spiritual healing. In v 7 the psalmist acknowledges God as a safe hiding place in a threefold statement of confidence that affirms the psalmist's trust that they are in right relationship with him.

The closing four verses (vv 8–11) are distinct from the rest of the psalm. They are presented as instruction. This, like the opening 'happy' (v 1) and the concern for the fate of the wicked, have often been understood to be wisdom themes found elsewhere in the Hebrew Bible. If this psalm was used liturgically in community worship, then we can either understand the psalmist to be instructing those listening, or see these words as God speaking through the psalmist. Verse 9 is an exhortation, a plea, to avoid being as stubborn as a mule, as the modern idiom goes.

Verse 10 carries the psalmist's basis for thanksgiving forward—the psalmist has moved from being one of the wicked to being one of the righteous, by confessing their sin. This saying reveals the psalmist's understanding of the way things are. Their view is part of a common biblical motif that human beings are either wicked or righteous. This notion underpins Psalms 1 and 119 already mentioned above. The contrast between the happy (vv 1 and 2) and the wicked reminds those that hear this psalm that the offer of mercy is best taken up immediately. This psalm captures the thanksgiving of the psalmist, who has received God's mercy, but also echoes the prophetic urgency seen elsewhere, for example in Isa 55.6–7.

Suggestions for Reflection and Discussion

- To what extent does Psalm 32 make sense as a sequel to Psalm 6?
- What do you make of the idea that unconfessed sin can give rise to physical ailments, as indicated in Ps 32.3?

Psalm 38

The previous psalm was a happy one. This psalm could not be more different. Although it is still beautiful, despite the horrors of the pain and suffering that it describes.

Psalm 38.1 is all but identical with that of Psalm 6.1.[24] In this way these two psalms are linked together. Unlike Psalm 6 its penitential nature is explicit—the psalmist both admits sinning (Ps 38.3–4) and is sorry for their sin (v 18).

This is further underlined in that God is said to be angry with the psalmist. This psalm also has all the hallmarks of a lament psalm. This means that we find the psalmist declaring the injustices perpetrated against them by their enemies, *eg* Ps 38.11–12.

Some interpreters understand the circumstances over which the psalmist laments as a natural part of being a penitent. Luther, for example, writes on this psalm with a self-understanding of first-hand chastisement by God for his sins, mediated through those who persecute him.[25] Such an interpretation sees, in all aspects of our suffering, the potential for God to chastise and transform us in our frailty. Of course, we need to be careful about cause and effect where sin and troubles are concerned—the Book of Job dismisses the notion of any consistent causal link between sin and suffering.

The structure of this psalm can be understood in different ways, but commentators agree that the bulk (vv 3–20) is framed by the first two verses and the last two verses. The opening singular address to God of 'O Lord' (v 1) is complemented by the warm and hopeful triple address to God in v 15:

> But it is for you, O Lord, that I wait;
>   it is you, O Lord my God, who will answer.

The ongoing wait is echoed poignantly at the psalm's close:

> Do not forsake me, O Lord;
>   O my God, do not be far from me;
> make haste to help me,
>   O Lord, my salvation. (vv 21–22)

The opening and closing sections form the overall plea within which we have the devastating and disturbing details of the psalmist's experiences. The psalmist faces hostility from their own community—friends, companions, neighbours (v 11). The psalm captures the pain of the psalmist, that those who are by the nature of their relationship closest, choose to stay at a distance. The dual attention to penitence and illness makes understanding the behaviour of the psalmist's community and family towards them difficult to pin down. This is typical of the openness of the psalms, already noted above with reference to their use of imagery. This, what we might term plasticity, makes this psalm valuable as a prayer in diverse contexts, not least as a penitential psalm.

Psalm 6 has a conclusion in which the psalmist trusts that God will restore them. Psalm 32 looks back, in thanksgiving, for a positive outcome of healing and forgiveness. There is no such resolution here in Psalm 38. For the psalmist, God appears to be silent, but they trust Yahweh resolutely by not equating his apparent passivity to their plight with absence. Like God, the psalmist's community also feel distant. With our limited contextual information and our knowledge of the gospel we want the psalmist's prayers to be answered. Are we as gracious to those struggling on the margins of our community when we know more details?

Having examined the first three penitential psalms it is apparent that they have some similar concerns. Collectively we could imagine someone going through a combination of illness and penitence, progressively praying and experiencing these psalms in the order Psalm 38, Psalm 6 and Psalm 32.

Suggestions for Reflection and Discussion

- List all the problems and ailments of the psalmist. To what extent are these to be understood metaphorically?
- Consider the psalm again, in what circumstances can you imagine using this as a personal prayer? How might you use it as a prayer for others?
- What factors might account for the penitential psalms being more marginal to faith today than in the medieval period?

3

Psalm 51: Lord, Have Mercy

Giving this psalm its own chapter draws attention to its role as the ultimate penitential psalm. As well as being known by its Latin opening, *Miserere mei, Deus* (Have mercy on me, O God) for some it is the 'Psalm of All Psalms.'[26] It lives up to this billing by virtue of its single-minded focus on penitence and the importance of the story, involving King David, that is traditionally taken to be at its heart.

Psalm 51

The biographical headings that reflect episodes in the life of King David appear at the head of thirteen psalms. They are almost universally judged to be late editorial additions by modern scholars. Nevertheless, such headings can still play an interpretive role in the canonical text due to their purposeful addition by the final collectors and editors of the psalter. The episode referred to at the head of Psalm 51 is arguably the lowest point of David's life. 2 Samuel 11–12 tells the story of sexual temptation, adultery with Bathsheba, the murder of her husband Uriah, and the prophet Nathan confronting David with his sin. In adding the heading to this psalm, the editors of the psalter provide a way to hear this psalm as David's prayer in addition to our using the psalm as our own words to God. Throughout the period in which the penitential psalms came to the fore in doctrine, piety and art, David's sin and subsequent penitence was understood as the context not only for this psalm but all seven penitential psalms. There is value in seeing it both with and without this interpretive lens.

Despite the horror and unwelcome intrusion of adultery and murder into the life of God's anointed there are, perhaps surprisingly, some positives. The narrative of 2 Samuel and the content of Psalm 51 remind us that God's boundless mercy can follow even the worst of sins. We have already seen the dramatic decisive willingness of God to forgive when David publicly acknowledges his sin (see Psalm 32 above). This is not simply good news for David, but good news for all. Augustine refers to this episode in a sermon and notes that we might not be sent a Nathan to prompt our confession, but we have been sent David so as to not fall in the first place.[27] This story, however, goes beyond personal piety. It raises interesting questions about the public role for confession and testimony. If confession is a hidden act are we not missing out on its potential value? As Wilson puts it, 'Plugging up the well—prevents others from drinking at the well of our experience and gaining the life-giving insights we have to offer.'[28] All of the penitential psalms we have looked at so far have a didactic (teaching and learning) trajectory to them.

As we work through Psalm 51, we will find that it offers other challenging insights into dealing with sin fully and appropriately. I will follow Wilson who understands this psalm to be comprised of six elements.[29]

The opening two verses capture the starkness of sinfulness and the hope of mercy with poetic beauty. Within them God is looked to for his 'mercy,' 'steadfast love' and 'abundant mercy,' the psalmist understands their wrongdoing as 'sin,' 'transgression' and 'iniquity,' and the anticipated action of God is to 'blot out,' 'wash,' and 'cleanse.' The psalmist understands the consequence of sin and wants restoration to right relationship with God. In traditional Davidic penitential readings, the reference to bloodguilt (v 14) is associated with Uriah's murder. Read more generically or liturgically this term can refer to our common frailty as fallen humanity.

The magnitude of the psalmist's sins is then unpacked in vv 3–6. The idea that David has sinned against God alone can, at first sight, grate given the consequences for Bathsheba and Uriah. We might also think that God's mercy is unseemly in its haste. After all Uriah is still dead and Bathsheba still David's wife. Of course, that is the very quality of mercy. If we hear these words as David's, we do not have to interpret them to mean he is ignoring the immediate human victims of his iniquity. Verses 3–5 are all about David looking at himself and asking just how deep and pervasive sin is. This problem is ever-present (v 3), it goes right back to the start of life (v 5), and at its worst it threatens whether life can be lived in relationship with the living God (v 4).

Verses 6–9 show that the psalmist wants more. They want to go beyond mercy and cleansing, to experience wholeness and restoration before God. There is immense hope for us all here. This is not simply the clean slate that blotting out might bring to mind. There is the promise of transformation through wisdom (v 6) at the deepest level of being—the psalmist's 'secret heart.' This is the possibility of gracious transformation or, as the New Testament explains it, sanctification.

The plea continues in vv 10–12 with the hope of spiritual cleansing and transformation. Again, we see a new beginning with the anticipation of something better, not just a 'right spirit' (v 10), but a 'willing spirit' (v 12) too. Verses 13–17 raise the issue of just what it means to be sorry for our sins—the need to go beyond just words. The psalm uses the metaphor of sacrifice, but the requirement is not a physical one but rather that of a broken spirit (v 17). The theological word sometimes used to describe this is contrition—in the NRSV the translators have paralleled 'contrite heart' with 'broken spirit.'

The last two verses of this psalm appear to be a late addition. The comments they make about burnt offerings and sacrifices might appear to be entirely at odds with v 16's claims. That there is some tension here is the case, and the late addition of these two verses might aim to a correct potential overzealous literal interpretation and the marginalization of the temple cult. The overall picture is that the psalmist sees beyond the ritual of sacrifice to the real issue for God—the need for genuine contrition.

Suggestions for Reflection and Discussion

- How would you break down this psalm into sections? What journey does this psalm take us on?
- Can we come before God, not only to find mercy and be cleansed, but to also be transformed? How can we best facilitate such cleansing and transformation?
- When, and how often, might you pray this psalm as your own words to God? [For centuries, many monks sang this psalm seven times each and every day!]

Psalms 102, 130 and 143: Hear My Prayer, O Lord

4

Two of the three final penitential psalms (Psalms 102 and 143) open with the words 'Hear my prayer, O Lord,' hence the title for this chapter. In liturgical use Psalms 102 and 143 are therefore known by the same Latin phrase: *Domine exaudi orationem meam*. Psalm 130 is known by the Latin title *De profundis* (out of the depths).

Psalm 102

In Psalm 102 we have a most earnest prayer from a psalmist suffering in a manner like the penitent of Psalm 32. Their ailments (Ps 102.3–5), literal or metaphorical, echo those seen in the first three penitential psalms (Pss 6.2; 32.3 and 38.3, 7). As we have come to expect by now the rich poetic imagery defies a monolithic interpretation—God, illness, and enemies all feature in the mix here.

In the thick of suffering a rational debate about cause and effect is not the priority. In fact, very often the psalms appear to display an intentional openness. The is an immense blessing when we turn to the psalms to use them as our own prayers.

Despite the painful plight of the poet this poem has a much broader concern beyond the life of the psalmist. Examining the structure of this psalm helps us appreciate this. Commentators agree that there are three main sections:[30]

- Psalm 102.1–11 are a lament right from the opening 'Hear my prayer, O Lord.'
- Verses 12–22 use hymn-like language to praise Yahweh.
- Verses 23–28 are a closing recapitulation of both the lament and praise.

Some interpreters find the juxtaposition of lament and praise odd and suggest that this is two older psalms joined as one. Whatever the textual history the three elements now work together coherently.

In the first section the words 'day' and 'days' feature four times (vv 2, 3, 8, 11), and this usage has been likened to a slowing heartbeat.[31] The word 'days' recapitulates in v 23. The temporal references in the middle section are of a different magnitude, emphasizing God's freedom from the constraints of time. Prior to v 12, the psalmist's illness and mortality seem to have been at the focus of the psalm. Verse 12 contrasts creaturely mortality with God as the one who is enthroned forever. God's unchanging nature is mentioned again towards the end of the psalm (v 27). Between vv 12 and 27, that each identify God as the eternal one, aspects of creation from the small scale to the cosmic, are seen to be transient or undergoing dramatic future change:

- The psalmist's imminent and premature death is evident in that they will not reach old age (v 24).
- Zion is a broken city (vv 13, 16–17), though it has a better future (v 21).
- God's people—the generations to come (v 18)—have a truly secure future (v 28).
- The nations have a future not as enemies but as people who will one day worship Israel's God (v 22).
- Even the heavens are limited in duration before the eternal God (vv 26–27).

The resolution of this lament differs from that in Psalm 6. In this case, the psalmist moves from introspection to the recognition that the whole of creation is in God's hand. Such a goal is, of course, where the trajectory of repentance ultimately must point. The other psalms we have looked at all have a move beyond themselves to other people who need to learn of God's mercy. Here, it is the new heaven and new earth, as a home for the faithful including the nations, that is the horizon of hope.

We also find in Psalm 102 evidence that the psalmist is penitent in the mention of tears and ashes in v 9. Although, this is only one way of reading these acts, they might simply be signs of lament. In adopting a penitential reading, we might imagine that the ashes play a sacramental role.

Ancient interpreters identify the three birds in this psalm respectively as pelican, owl, and sparrow. The NRSV translates the Hebrew as owl, little owl and lonely bird. The difficulty in pinning down the Hebrew here has led to some odd reflections over the years, including a myth that pelicans kill their young and resurrect them three days later. The point, however, seems to be an empathetic and poetic illustration of loneliness—the psalmist is alone, like any number of solitary birds, and v 8 brings this ornithological poetry home with a punch. This loneliness and rejection fits with the all too frequent experience of those suffering with wrongdoing and/or illness.[32]

Ancient interpreters do not just disagree with modern interpreters over the identity of the birds. They are often quicker to find Christ in the psalms than we are. Augustine typifies this in his Psalms commentary, comprised largely of sermons, where he sees Christ everywhere throughout the psalter. In a classic preacher's ploy Augustine refuses to identify who the psalmist is in Psalm 102—it is self-evidently Christ for Augustine. His audience know, and he knows that they know he knows, it is Christ.[33] He plays a game for minutes of his sermon—teasing his congregation mercilessly. Even penitential psalms can be spoken by the sinless Christ. He prays these words on behalf of his body the church.[34]

Suggestions for Reflection and Discussion

- Just how much freedom do we have to inhabit these words and make them ours?
- What evidence is there within this psalm that the psalmist is nearing the end of their life? Do we miss something vital in testifying to Christ in our culture because both it, and we, are so reticent about discussing death?
- What possibilities and value exist in seeing Christ as the psalmist in Psalm 102?

Psalm 130

Psalm 130 is not only one of the seven penitential psalms, it is also one of the fifteen psalms of ascents. Like its neighbours it is short, the shortest of the penitential psalms. Despite its brevity it has immense value and its succinct poetry makes it a composition of profound beauty.

In the Hebrew text 'the depths' are the unfathomable depths of the ocean. The metaphorical meaning is the place of turmoil in life where we are dragged down, whether it be by sin, anxiety, depression, illness, worry or oppression. This imagery works for us today as a metaphor, but in biblical culture this concept was richer and profoundly theological. The depths of the sea are a place of chaos where things are disordered (Isa 51.9–10). The prophet Jonah famously manages to live out this metaphor in the belly of a fish having run away from God (Jonah 2.2–3). In Jonah the connection is made with *sheol*, the grave, a place where the dead await the end of the age as shades of their former selves (so Prov 9.18), cut off from God and unable to remember or praise him, as we saw in Ps 6.5 in our first study.

Despite the difficulties facing the psalmist, or perhaps because of them, the psalmist shapes their prayer eloquently. Its eight verses form four two-verse strophes:[35]

- Strophe 1: Ps 130.1–2. A cry to God.
- Strophe 2: vv 3–4. A statement of confidence.
- Strophe 3: vv 5–6. Waiting for the Lord.
- Strophe 4: vv 7–8. The redemption of Israel.

This psalm exemplifies the profound trust that is a key characteristic of the Psalter. Having cried to God in desperate need (vv 1–2) the psalmist is confident that God has not only heard but will forgive (vv 3–4). It is this confidence that appears to sustain them in their waiting (vv 5–6). Perhaps they are awaiting a sign that acknowledges that their iniquities will no longer be counted, or marked (v 3)? Or maybe, like the psalmist elsewhere, there is an anxiety or illness which the psalmist wants rid of? Perhaps it is simply the sense of expectation of a new day before God, no longer burdened with the weight of guilt obscuring a right relationship with the Lord?

Whatever the psalmist hopes for the poetry is poignant. In the space of two verses, vv 5–6, the psalmist is consistently and determinedly waiting, watching and hoping for the Lord. Some of the phrases are repeated, such as 'more than those who watch for the morning.' This poetic device is frequently used in the psalms of ascents and here it heightens the sense of anticipation. This specific metaphor simultaneously refers to those that would guard the city overnight, who would have breathed a sigh of relief that the safer daylight hours have arrived without event, and the expectation that God does new things at first light. This verse can take on a new dynamic when we remember the story of Jesus' resurrection (Mark 16.2).

The sense of waiting is heightened further by the repetition of 'my soul waits' (vv 5 and 6). The word 'soul,' here in the NRSV and many modern English versions, translates the Hebrew word *nepeš*. As Goldingay helpfully explains this 'is a word of wide-ranging meaning. It can denote the person as a whole, or the person's inner being, outer being, or life…it is misleading to think of *nepeš* as denoting the soul as the real person within a disposable shell called the body.'[36] 'Very being' is perhaps a helpful English equivalence in capturing the sense of the earnestness and trust of the psalmist here.

We have seen on several occasions now that the penitential psalms tend to have some movement beyond the psalmist. This can concern the salvation, judgment, and/or teaching of others. In this case the redemption of all Israel is the concluding prospect. This hope for Zion might well stem from the same tragedy we met in the previous studies on Psalms 51 and 102. There Jerusalem had broken walls (Ps 51.18) and scattered people (Ps 102.16–17). Like the psalmist, the troubles of Jerusalem and her people are the result of God's chastisement, and they will be over on the day of redemption. This side of Easter, we know that this redemption comes through the one who journeyed to Jerusalem and proclaimed, 'This is my blood of the covenant, which is poured out for many for the forgiveness of sins' (Matt 26.28).[37]

Suggestions for Reflection and Discussion

- Have you personally experienced the depths? In what way did you, or do you, experience them?
- What burdens can you bring before God by praying this psalm? What does it mean to wait upon God after we bring our burdens to him? Do we find this difficult?
- Imagine Jesus praying this psalm in Gethsemane. How does this psalm function and feel when we read the words as Christ praying?

Psalm 143

Having reflected on the first six penitential psalms this psalm feels familiar. Like Psalms 38 and 102 it is a lament psalm. Its only reference to penitence is Ps 143.2 where the psalmist freely acknowledges their lack of righteousness before a righteous God. The rest of the psalm is concerned with deliverance from enemies (vv 3, 9, 11 and 12) and the psalmist's desire for God's instruction (vv 8 and 10).

Verse 7 can be understood as the centre of the psalm. Prior to this verse the psalmist's concern has been expressed as the need for deliverance from 'the enemy.' Here the psalmist expresses most profoundly their underlying plight as the perceived absence of God:

> Answer me quickly, O Lord; [a]
>   my spirit fails. [b]
> Do not hide your face from me, [c]
>   or I shall be like those who go down to the Pit. [d]
>
> Ps 143.7, NRSV

In v 7 we see that the psalmist wants to be delivered from going down to the pit, a metaphor for *sheol* (v 7d). This echoes the psalmist calling from the depths which we saw in the previous section on Psalm 130. This stresses that the concerns of the poet are life and death matters. It is little wonder that the psalmist wants an answer urgently (v 7a), and that their spirit is failing (v 7b).

The psalmist feels that God is remote from their plight (v 7c), and in this dire emergency, they tell Yahweh they fear imminent death (v 7d).

Reference to God's face echoes the use of the same metaphor in Ps 102.2. In Psalm 51 we saw the psalmist petitioning God that he would hide his face from their sin (Ps 51.9), suggesting that they were experiencing God's face turned towards them. If we look beyond the penitential psalms to the rest of the Psalter, this motif is very common in the psalms. In the first 25 psalms alone the presence, or absence, of God's face is mentioned seven times: Pss 4.6; 10.11; 11.7; 13.1; 17.15; 22, 24; 24.6. The ubiquity of this imagery in the psalter is related to its centrality to the Aaronic blessing (Num 6.24–26):

> The Lord bless you and keep you;
> the Lord make his face to shine upon you, and be gracious to you;
> the Lord lift up his countenance upon you, and give you peace.

The psalmist is desperate to experience this reality once again. Some have suggested that the seven psalms are like seven steps on a ladder. This has not been evident in our journey—and surely it would be odd if it were. Why should we expect an end to this journey of setting aside our sin? Only when we ourselves end up in the 'world to come' will our need to pray for forgiveness and cleansing have gone. Contrary to arriving at a special place of blessing we can see that the seven penitential psalms end rather bleakly. Not only is the psalmist still lamenting illness, spiritual depression, and enemies, but they finish by wishing that their enemies would be destroyed (Ps 143.12).

Of course, our goal was not a naïve expectation of a single journey but familiarization with one part of the Scriptures that are our constant companion on the way. In the closing chapter we consider this role of the penitential psalms today.

Suggestions for Reflection and Discussion

- To what extent does the image of God's face shining on us work today?
- What does the psalmist mean when they say that their soul thirsts for God like a parched land? To what extent do the psalms function in the life of faith as diagnosis and remedy?

Using the Penitential Psalms Today

5

The seven psalms help us appreciate the seriousness of sin. A penitential reading of these psalms permits us to see that Christ is the enabler of the salvation, cleansing and deliverance spoken of in these wonderful poems. The penitential psalms testify to the ongoing need to deal with our frailty and failings. They can be an important part of a healthy spirituality that takes spiritual growth seriously by acknowledging the debilitating effects of sin and guilt.

We have seen that despite being scattered throughout the psalter these seven psalms have a complex relationship with one another. They share, at the literary level, a variety of motifs and ideas:

- This is the language of the soul, heart and spirit—the whole person: see Pss 6.3; 32.2; 38.8; 51.6; 102.4; 130.5 and 143.6–7.
- There is the spiritual angst that manifests itself physically in a variety of ways, including in one's bones, as in Pss 6.2; 38.3; 51.8 and 102.3.
- The longing for deliverance and an experience of God's presence, seen in Pss 6.4; 32.7; 38.22; 51.14; 102.2; 130.8 and 143.11.
- The recognition that we wait before the living God in trust, as seen in Pss 6.3; 38.15; 130.5–6 and 143.8.

These seven psalms provide the vocabulary of a serious faith that is concerned with spiritual and physical health, what it means to live well before God, and the recognition that relationship with God enables living life to the full. Of course, they are not unique in this. The raw spirituality they testify to, and the motifs listed above, connect them with the lament psalms that make up around a third of the psalter. In recent years there has been something of a recovery of the lament tradition. It is my hope that the penitential psalms would also be known and used more widely, to ensure that we use the psalms to call to God in bold language, not only that we might voice our petitions, but also deal with the most fundamental challenge that can hold us back on our walk with Christ.

The penitential psalms not only testify to the heart of Christian faith, but they also remind us that we have a testimony that should manifest itself in evangelism. These often grim psalms are not bad news; they are the offer of the good news of spiritual health lived in Christ. This experience that we know as penitents is the tangible lived-out gospel hope that we can offer to others. These seven psalms represent and testify to our transformation. They have the gospel potential to transform—to enable the journey from sinner to penitent to disciple to disciple-maker.

In closing we can briefly comment on the lack of prominence of the penitential psalms today. Why was is that what were once the most utilized psalms of the Middle Ages were eclipsed by others? As we have already mentioned, a penitential lens is but one interpretive approach. Lenses open our eyes only to the extent of their focus. A penitential lens was especially coherent with the religious sensibilities of the medieval period in the light of doctrinal developments around Lenten practice and especially the doctrines of purgatory and penance. Until recently, historical-critical scholarship has been wary of reading the Old Testament with any approach other than those centred on historical reconstructions. Reading the psalms in their complex historical, cultic and literary context is, of course, a rich and vital endeavour. Nevertheless, a penitential reading is not only part of the wider family of Christian theological readings but is closer to some Jewish readings than is sometimes appreciated. Recently attention has been drawn to the rise of penitential prayer in post-exilic Israel. Just as we celebrated Psalm 51 as the penitential psalm *par excellence* above, some scholars have identified this psalm as evidence of the importance of a penitential interpretive approach in the post-exilic period, the time the psalter was being edited into its final form.[38]

I hope that some readers of this booklet will want to use it as the basis for a Lent study group, or similar. It can be adapted from its current structure in several ways depending on the context. I have found that a series of three studies based respectively on chapters 2, 3 and 4 works well.

Further Reading

Anyone wanting to explore the penitential psalms at the height of their popularity and importance will find the following an engaging and delightful overview:

> C Costley King'oo, *Misere Mei: The Penitential Psalms in Late Medieval and Early Modern England* (Notre Dame, IN: University of Notre Dame Press, 2012).

For those interested in how the category of penitential psalms works with modern classification of the psalms this is a valuable technical work:

H P Nasuti, *Defining the Sacred Songs: Genre, Tradition, and the Post-Critical Interpretation of the Psalms* (Sheffield: Sheffield Academic Press, 1999).

Further Listening

Whether you go on to lead a group study or have simply read this booklet for your own interest I would encourage you to explore some of the music that has arisen from the penitential psalms. The examples here were introduced in chapter one:

A crisp profound version of Allegri's *Miserere Mei* can be found on VOCES8, *Lux* (Decca, 2015).

Arvo Pärt's challenging take on Psalm 51 is found with two other choral works on Arvo Pärt, *Miserere* (ECM New Series, 2000).

Three penitential psalms (51, 102 and 130), among other psalms, can be found on Howard Goodall, *Pelican in the Wilderness: Songs from the Psalms* (Classic FM, 2010).

Leonard Cohen's riff on Psalm 51 can be found on Leonard Cohen, *The Essential Leonard Cohen* (Columbia Records, 1992).

Notes

1 The Greek (LXX) and Latin (Vulgate) traditions number the penitential psalms as Psalm 6, 31, 37, 50, 101, 129 and 142. This is because, among other differences, Psalms 9 and 10 in the Hebrew Masoretic text are a single psalm, numbered 9, in both the Greek and Latin versions.

2 H P Nasuti, *Defining the Sacred Songs: Genre, Tradition, and the Post-Critical Interpretation of the Psalms* (Sheffield: Sheffield Academic Press, 1999) p 33.

3 Cassiodorus, *Explanation of the Psalms*, 3 volumes, P G Walsh (trans) (New York: Paulist Press, 1990).

4 S Gillingham, *Psalms through the Centuries: Volume 1* (Oxford: Blackwell, 2008) p 113.

5 A Barratt (ed), *The Seven Psalms: A Commentary on the Penitential Psalms Translated from French into English by Dame Eleanor Hull* (Oxford University Press, 1995).

6 C Costley King'oo, *Misere Mei: The Penitential Psalms in Late Medieval and Early Modern England* (Notre Dame, IN: University of Notre Dame Press, 2012) p 26.

7 *ibid,* pp 41–52.

8 B W Anderson and S Bishop, *Out of the Depths: The Psalms Speak for Us Today*, third edition (Louisville, KY: Westminster John Knox Press, 2000) p 78.

9 N deClassié-Walford, R A Jacobson and B LaNeel Tanner, *The Book of Psalms* (Grand Rapids, MI: Eerdmans, 2014) p 929.

10 Nasuti, *Sacred Songs, op cit,* p 37.

11 S E Ballentine, '"I Was Ready to be Sought Out by Those Who do not Ask,"' pp 1–20 in M J Boda *et al, Seeking the Favor of God Volume 1: The Origins of Penitential Prayer in Second Temple Judaism* (Atlanta, GA: Society of Biblical Literature, 2006) p 2.

12 M Luther, *Werke, Tischreden 1531–46,* 1st Book (Weimar: Hermann Böhlaus Nachfolger, 1912) p 375.

13 J Fisher, *Exposition of the Seven Penitential Psalms*, A Barbeau Gardiner (trans) (San Francisco, CA: Ignatius Press, 1998) p xxiii.

14 P M George, *The Sacramental Art of John Donne's Sermons on the Penitential Psalms*, PhD thesis (The University of British Columbia, 1996) p 3.

15 P M George, *The Sacramental Art of John Donne's Sermons on the Penitential Psalms, op cit, passim.*

16 G Herbert, *The Complete Poetry* (London: Penguin Books, 2015) p 102.

17 Gillingham, *Psalms through the Centuries, op cit,* p 184.

18 J M Neale and R F Littledale, *A Commentary on the Psalms: From Primitive and Mediaeval Writers* volume 1 (London: Joseph Masters, second edition, 1869) p 124.

19 R Alter, *The Book of Psalms: A Translation with Commentary* (New York: W W Norton and Company, 2007).

20 E T Charry, *Psalms 1–50* (Grand Rapids, MI: Brazos Press, 2015) p 27.

21 Commentators differ on how this psalm should be broken into strophes. Here I follow J Goldingay, *Psalms Volume 1: Psalms 1–41* (Grand Rapids, MI: Baker

Academic, 2006) pp 134–135. See E T Charry, *Psalms 1–50, op cit,* p 28 and N deClassié-Walford *et al, The Book of Psalms, op cit,* p 102 for two alternatives.

22 J Goldingay, *Psalms Volume 1, op cit,* p 137.

23 W Brueggemann and W H Bellinger, *Psalms: New Cambridge Commentary* (Cambridge University Press, 2014) p 161 note this feature of the dialogue between David and Nathan shown here.

24 There is, in fact, a very minor difference in the Hebrew but this is so small that it is not reflected in either the NRSV or NIV.

25 For example, see Luther, *LW 14,* p 155.

26 S Gillingham, *Psalms through the Centuries: Volume 2* (Oxford: Blackwell, 2018) pp 304–316.

27 Augustine, *Expositions of the Psalms, volume 2,* M Boulding (trans), J E Rotelle (ed) (Hyde Park, NY: New City Press, 2000) p 414.

28 G H Wilson, *Psalms Volume 1* (Grand Rapids, MI: Zondervan, 2002) p 783.

29 *ibid,* p 773.

30 So, for example, S Terrien, *The Psalms: Strophic Structure and Theological Commentary* (Grand Rapids, MI: Eerdmans, 2003) pp 694–696.

31 W D Tucker Jr and J A Grant, *Psalms 2* (Grand Rapids, MI: Zondervan, 2018) p 471.

32 S Terrien, *The Psalms, op cit,* p 697.

33 I am indebted to J Byassee, *Psalms 101–150* (Grand Rapids, MI: Brazos Press, 2018) p 6 for this point. See Augustine, *Expositions of the Psalms, volume 5 ,* M Boulding (trans), J E Rotelle (ed) (Hyde Park, NY: New City Press, 2003) 5 pp 45–47.

34 See J F Wellington, *Praying the Psalms with Jesus: A Journey of Discovery and Recognition* (Grove Spirituality booklet S132) for a short introduction to finding Christ in the Psalms and J Byassee, *Praise Seeking Understanding: Reading the Psalms with Augustine* (Grand Rapids, MI: Eerdmans, 2007) for the concept of the *totus Christus* in Augustine's christological ecclesiology.

35 The headings of the four strophes here are lightly adapted from Tucker and Grant, *Psalms 2, op cit,* pp 821–825. N deClassié-Walford *et al, The Book of Psalms, op cit,* p 926 proposes very similar headings for these four strophes.

36 J Goldingay, *Psalms Volume 3, op cit,* p 759.

37 J Byassee, *Psalms 101–150, op cit,* p 160 makes this helpful connection.

38 See, for example, J L Mays, *Psalms: Interpretation Bible Commentary* (Louisville, KY: John Knox Press, 1994, p 145 and R Bautsch, '"May Your Eyes Be Open and Your Ears Attentive": A Study of Penance and Penitence in the Writings,' pp 67–85 in M J Boda, *Repentance in Christian Theology* (Collegeville, MN: Liturgical Press, 2006) p 70.